CW00321437

PENNY BLACK'S
CARDS
AND
COLLAGES

PENNY BLACK'S
CARDS
AND
COLLAGES

Photographs by
JACQUI HURST

EBURY PRESS LONDON

First published in 1993 by Ebury Press
an imprint of Random House UK Ltd
Random House
20 Vauxhall Bridge Road
London SW1V 2SA

Text copyright © Penny Black 1993
Photographic copyright © Random House UK Ltd 1993

Penny Black has asserted her right to be identified
as the author of this work in accordance with the
Copyright, Designs and Patents Act 1988.

All rights reserved. No part of this publication
may be reproduced, stored in a retrieval system,
or transmitted in any form or by any means,
electronic, mechanical, photocopying, recording
or otherwise, without the prior permission
of the copyright owners.

A catalogue record for this book is available
from the British Library.

ISBN 0 09 177357 1

Editor: Gillian Haslam
Design: Polly Dawes
Illustrations: Dennis Curran

Typeset by Textype Typesetters, Cambridge
Printed and bound in Italy by
New Interlitho S.p.a., Milan

SUPPLIERS

Jill Cadnam, 6 The Old Boys' School,
Illogan, Churchtown, Redruth, Cornwall TR16 4SW
(Handmade Indian papers)

Arts and Graphics, 4 West End, Redruth,
Cornwall TR15 2RZ Tel: 0209 211222
(Papers and art materials)

Falkiner Fine Papers Ltd, 76 Southampton Row,
London WC1 Tel: 071 831 1151
(Papers and art materials)

The endpaper is reproduced courtesy of Falkiner
Fine Papers and manufacturer Richard de Bas.

CONTENTS

❧ INTRODUCTION ❧

THE first printed card, conveying a message of congratulations, was printed in 1829. The first Christmas card was sent by Henry Cole, the founder of the Victoria and Albert museum, in 1843. Picture postcards were printed when the introduction of the railway system enabled more people to participate in family holidays, particularly those by the sea. When the penny post came into operation the whole business of sending cards burgeoned and by the 1890s they were being mass-produced in their thousands by the company Raphael Tuck. The sending of valentine cards, picture postcards, cards celebrating anniversaries, festivals and announcements, communications, messages and invitations and, of course, the writing of letters became a way of life for most people.

This social communication continues just as avidly today and it is an important aspect of our lives, reinforcing and perpetuating the relationships we have with our family and friends and establishing a rapport with those whom we previously did not know. In recent years pretty and decorative cards have become popular and in our busy society, with less and less free time for letter-writing, a few lines written on a well chosen card can be just as pleasurable to receive as the conventional letter, perhaps more so if the card is propped up where it can be admired. My cards live on the mantelshelf in the kitchen where they remind me of my family and friends. Periodically I am forced to have a clear-out, but can never bring myself to discard them and consequently cards erupt from all my dresser drawers. Such is the popularity of cards today!

Many people may wish to use this book as a guideline and as inspiration for making cards for family and friends, but some may wish to make cards on a commercial basis. If you are not already experienced in the craft, it is essential to get as much practice as quickly as possible. There is little point in launching into the creation of the most elaborate card as the first project – it is better by far to move with caution and start experimenting with the very basic Botanical Cards on p.64. They require little experience and will give the initial surge of enthusiasm that is necessary to continue. If the advice provided in this book is followed, then those very first attempts should look quite professional and more elaborate cards can follow. Over a period of just a few days expertise will grow and so, subconsciously, will an eye for colour and balance.

It is not necessary to have an extensive supply of pressed botanicals, for they can be supplemented with fragrant spices from the kitchen cupboard, seeds, ribbons and threads, and any tiny beads or sequins that are available. None of the collages in this book should prove too difficult to make, but it is most important to adopt a very lateral approach to a craft that in the past has had a very limited application; never be nervous of experimenting with any pretty snippet of anything that could enhance the artistry and interest of a collage. Of course the collages decorating these cards can easily be expanded to make larger pictures and, once experience has been gained, this becomes the natural progression, if you have the desire to attempt more demanding work.

I enjoy making cards immensely and find they are the ideal way in which to experiment with style, colour and new ideas. I am a firm believer that all those who love flowers and the natural landscape possess an innate artistic ability and in many of us this remains dormant. I made my first pressed flower picture only seven years ago and although it was sadly lacking in artistry, it aroused in me a suspicion that perhaps I was capable of more. I experimented in all directions and with the manipulation of the smallest jot of craft I began to unravel an art form that now captivates me. In creating the cards in this book I have been able to experiment with all sorts of notions and I hope that they will set readers on the path to discovering more for themselves.

❧ PAPERS ❧

Over the past few years I have amassed a wide and rich collection of papers. When I first started making my collages I knew nothing of hand-made paper and I only used good quality machine-made paper as a background. However, while browsing in an arts and crafts shop one day I came upon a drawer of hand-made papers. I was immediately fascinated by their tactile rough texture and appealing ragged edges and bought a single sheet with which to experiment. So began an interest in hand-made papers, their romantic history and a strong desire to make my own one day. I also began to appreciate and learn more about machine-made papers and along my journey of discovery have experimented in all sorts of directions, finding ways in which to divide, colour and use both machine-made and hand-made papers. I now place as much importance on the paper I use as on the botanicals that will decorate it.

Like many of the ancient crafts, paper-making has a romantic history. It originated in China some 2000 years ago and the documented invention is attributed to Ts'ai Lun, a Chinese eunuch, who is credited with making the first paper pulp in the year 105 AD. He used a maceration of natural fibrous materials that included barks, hemp, linen and cotton rags and other plant materials, eventually deciding upon old rags as being the best components. Paper-making remained the secret of the Chinese for hundreds of years but it eventually reached Japan in the eighth century AD where the Empress Shotuka commissioned *The Million Prayers*, the first known text to be printed on paper. It was also during this century that the secret of paper-making spread through the Muslim world to Samarkand and then on to Baghdad, Damascus and Cairo. During the twelfth century the Moors carried the craft to Spain and Portugal, but it was not established in Christendom until the thirteenth century. Many of the plants that had been used for paper-making in Asia were not available in Europe and initially paper was made from cotton and linen rags. However, with the development of the printing trade, and the demand for paper, in the early nineteenth century there began a search for a more plentiful raw material and this led to the discovery of wood pulp.

Today most of our paper is made from wood pulp and of course all paper used commercially is machine-made. Fortunately for artists and craftspeople hand-made paper is still available. A few old established companies in Europe still use the old hand method of paper-making and there are individual craftspeople who make and sell beautiful papers. However, it is from the Third World that most of our hand-made papers now come. Almost any fibrous materials can be used for paper-making and from the leaves of the water hyacinth, the trimmings of silk fabrics and jute carpets, intriguing and individual papers are being made. Many of these papers are made solely from recycled waste. I am fascinated by the variations in their thickness and texture, never minding at all if a sturdy paper dwindles to a mere tissue in places, or that the deckle-edges may display a border reminiscent of that on an old frayed blanket. This adds to the character and individuality of hand-made paper. Some papers have whole flowers, petals, seeds, ferns, grasses and tufts of wool, silk and cotton as an intrinsic part of their fabric, whilst others may only be speckled with seaweed, algae, straw, husks or tea. Colours are as diverse as textures and I particularly love the manilla browns, sepia, ochre, sandy, ivory and occasionally chalk white papers. Some of the acrylic colours of the dyed papers are fun to work with, as are finely marbled papers.

Machine-made papers also have a role, for they can be colourwashed, shaded with pastels, gilded and painted. They can even be made to look like hand-made paper if the edges of a sheet of white paper are hand-torn and the paper brushed with cold tea. These papers come in all weights and colours and it is worth examining everything, even black paper can be used. But the ultimate in convenience is a pad of white watercolour or Ingres pastel papers. The sheets measure about 6×9in (15×22½cm) which, when folded, is an appropriate size for a card. These are excellent papers to use as basic cards, for not everyone is inclined towards deckle-edges and fancy papers.

Although papers do vary in weight, this never really concerns me. If a paper is too thick to fold properly then just a single card can be made or a sheet of the thick paper glued to the front of a basic card, if it is transparent or insubstantial then a sheet of this too can be lightly glued to the front of a basic card. It is the visual impact of paper that should dictate how it is used and any problem regarding weight can be overcome. However, if machine-made paper is being used for a large quantity of cards, I would recommend medium- to light-weight.

Of course there are many papers that I have not mentioned and it is a case of keeping an opportunistic eye open. White ceiling papers and some wallpapers can make interesting cards, as can brown manilla and wrapping paper. All sorts of possibilities abound and they are all part and parcel of the hunt for treasure. I have become fascinated by paper but perhaps this is understandable for it is, after all, just another aspect of our use of the botanical kingdom.

THE equipment needed for making these cards and collages can be quite basic, but if more elaborate techniques are to be used for applying backgrounds, then the list of paints, pastels, polishes, brushes, pens and draughtsman's equipment can be quite extensive. It is best to start off with the bare necessities and gradually add to the collection as the inclination to experiment develops.

The first tool to acquire is a pair of surgical forceps. Whether dealing with fresh botanicals for pressing or dry ones for use in a collage, it is advisable to manipulate everything with forceps. Fragile botanicals are easily damaged by handling and the sooner one becomes accustomed to the use of forceps, the better. Small seeds, spices, beads and berries are almost impossible to place by hand but with forceps they can be quite firmly gripped, dipped in glue and then placed in position. Orange sticks are required as in most cases one will be used to dab the glue on the back of the botanicals. Of course you need a ruler, pencil, rubber and a pair of scissors for measuring the card and trimming the botanicals. Lastly, and perhaps a luxury, I do suggest that all writing is done with the finest of draughtsman's pens; it is important that the end result of your labours should have a professional appearance and the use of the correct pen will complete this impression.

I believe that interesting backgrounds and colourwashed papers and cards can completely change the visual impact of botanical pictures. I use all sorts of mediums to create the desired effect. Watercolours are an obvious choice, as are the coloured inks. Soft pastels produce gentle colours and I particularly like the iridescent ones. I rub them on paper and then smudge the colours with a fingertip and a stroke or two of oil pastel, either in the same colour or a toning shade. All sorts of beautiful effects can be achieved in this way. Wax crayons and coloured pencils can be used, but again I like to mix them with soft pastels.

Non-tarnishing wax gilt is available in most craft shops and its uses are inexhaustible. The polish smears perfectly over smooth papers and textured papers are left dappled gold. Metallic paints give a dense covering on paper and they are excellent to use when a narrow border is required. Gold and silver watercolours are fascinating and I find the suspension of metallic colour in water can give the most delicate iridescent effect when brushed onto card. Lustre powders and glitter can be sprinkled onto any surface covered with adhesive. Sheets of real gold and silver leaf are a complete luxury but I do use them occasionally as the effect is exquisite. Gold and silver spray paint is useful, particularly when botanicals need to be gilded.

A draughtsman's propelling pencil can save the fiddle of sharpening and once acquired should last a lifetime. Narrow gold and silver pens are useful and so, too, are the wider acrylic felt tip pens. Paint brushes fascinate me although I am not an artist – I use them in variety for watercolours, distributing lustre powder and glitter, spreading glue, applying polish and wax and sweeping away fragments of debris from a collage. It is good to amass a wide collection of all sizes for they will all have their use.

Glues are always a vexed question and there are many to choose from. I work with just a few and by far the most used is an ordinary rubber-based glue – it can always be rubbed or pulled off paper, the back of botanicals and even oneself if necessary. I have recently discovered PVA glue and I use it diluted to paint over flat botanicals that need some form of protection against rough handling, and also as an adhesive for glitter and lustre powders. I use writers' gold size as an adhesive for gold and silver gilt and also to increase the transparency of tissue paper. It can also be painted over flat botanicals for protection. Spray glue also has its uses, particularly when a very fragile surface has to be covered with an adhesive.

A good pair of craft scissors will make life easier when cutting card and botanicals, as will a craft knife. A professional bone folder is easier to use than any substitute and I am extremely fond of my old one, but they are not easy to come by.

Finally, I would like to suggest that everyone has a magnifying glass to hand, for all my work has been inspired by a love of flowers and a detailed study of the botanical world.

MAKING CARDS

RATHER than buying commercially manufactured blank cards which are available in most craft shops, I prefer to make my own, choosing the paper that will most enhance my collage. Hand-made papers have immense appeal and character, but machine-made can also make excellent cards. The most important thing is how one treats the papers and what kind of cards are made.

Most of my cards and small gift tags are folded, but they can quite easily be made on single sheets of paper with the message written on the back of the design.

Cutting and tearing the paper that will be used for cards is most important and should be done well. After the paper has been measured to size, and the guidelines drawn, it can be either carefully cut with scissors, or, even better, with a guillotine if available. If using a guillotine, it is easier to cut several cards of the same size from one large sheet of paper. If possible I like to use the natural deckle-edge of hand-made paper on at least one side of my cards. This means that the remaining edges must be hand-torn and I have devised the following methods for doing this.

METHOD 1 – FOR ALL PAPERS
1 Fold the paper along pencil guidelines.

2 With a ruler ⅛in (2mm) from the fold, run a bone folder along the fold several times.

3 Unfold paper and carefully tear along fold.

METHOD 2 – FOR MOST PAPERS, APART FROM VERY THICK ONES
1 Take a draughtsman's propelling pencil and ensure that the lead is fully retracted.

2 Place a ruler along the pencil guideline and run the metal tip of pencil along it until there is a semi-perforated groove on the paper.

3 Carefully pull paper apart along groove.

METHOD 3 – FOR THICKER PAPER ONLY
1 Immerse paper on which guidelines have been drawn in water until it is saturated. Remove and dab dry with a paper towel or cloth.

2 Loosely fold along pencil guidelines. Unfold and carefully tear apart. Lay on flat surface to dry. This method gives an excellent deckle-edge.

HOW TO FOLD CARD PROFESSIONALLY
1 Fold rectangle of card in half.

2 Place a ruler ⅛in (2mm) from edge of the fold and, holding it firmly in place with one hand and holding a bone folder (or knife handle) with the other hand, run the flat end of the bone folder firmly along the edge of the card along the edge of the ruler, flattening and sharpening the fold.

3 Keep the ruler in the same place and using the pointed end of the bone folder and pressing firmly run it along ruler thereby giving the edge of the flattened fold a finishing ridge.

4 If desired, this technique may also be used to flatten the outer edges of the card.

At the beginning of the list of materials, given in the instructions on how to make various cards, I have always given the measurement of a card when folded. To work out the unfolded measurement simply double the length of the edge that runs up to the fold.

With few exceptions I use rubber-based glue when constructing my collages. As the botanicals will not normally have any protective covering over them they must be glued in place quite firmly, but must never lose their natural line. Nothing is more unattractive than a heavily glued picture. All stalks, leaves and buds should have their reverse side covered with small dots of glue applied with an orange stick ½in (1cm) apart. Very small flowers and buds only need one dot of glue applied to their reverse centre and larger flowers should have a dot applied to the centre of the outer edge of the petals, ¹⁄₁₆in (1mm) from the edge, as well. Seeds, berries and spices can be held by forceps and just dipped into glue and then placed in position. The same applies to beads, sequins and shells. Any ribbons, threads or braids should only be glued in place where absolutely necessary, or their natural appearance will disappear. Occasionally I do use PVA glue for the adhesion of lustre powders and glitter to a background. Spray glue is useful for covering the entire surface of a fragile botanical that must be very securely fixed; this particularly applies to skeletonised leaves.

I have never used any form of plastic film to cover the collages on my cards, which is why I take care over the method of gluing. I cannot come to terms with this product and feel that it destroys the natural feel of my work and my collages are often too textured for it to work properly in any case. However, there are methods of protecting the flatter collages which I occasionally use. Diluted PVA glue can be brushed over

botanical decorations and this will give a most subtle protection which is totally invisible. Writer's gold size can also be brushed over them and although this is slightly visible, it does not give an unacceptable finish. The same also applies to aerosol matt polyurethane. Occasionally I do dip my cards in melted wax which gives a charming result for the paper takes on the appearance of vellum and the flowers are discreetly veiled by the wax. A warning note is that lots of practice is needed and every fire precaution must be taken as wax is highly inflammable.

There are a few rules on balance that I have discovered through trial and error, only to have found out later that these rules are, in fact, observed by most artists. Any decorative collage should be positioned slightly towards the top of its background, and if the decorated background is then to be mounted on the front of a card, then this also should be positioned slightly towards the top of the card. This also means that if the collage is signed or named then the general impression remains balanced. The difference may only be a matter of a millimetre or two, but the difference in perspective is quite marked.

INGREDIENTS

Part of the fun of making these cards and collages is the collecting of the ingredients. I certainly have the instincts of a magpie and almost every receptacle in the cottage has its occupants. Mirror-glass from India lives in a Davenport tea cup, cowry shells in a tiny jug, ribbons in a basket hanging from a beam and sequins and beads in a glass vase where I can see my collection at a glance.

The most important components of these collages are the pressed botanicals and with the exception of some tropical fruit and vegetables, nearly all can be gathered from the garden and countryside. Small rosebuds are invaluable and I grow *Rosa multiflora* and *Rosa farreri persetosa*. I also like to dry and press larger old roses. I am constantly using the round blossoms of all the shrubby and herbaceous potentillas. Astilbes, anaphalis, anemones, blue- and pinkbells, feverfew, pink and white *Polygonum campanulatum*, celandines, buttercups, dandelions, lilac, forget-me-nots, elder flowers and various clematis are some of the smaller flowers I find most useful.

I prefer to use only small leaves and so I press *Rosa farreri persetosa*, herbaceous geranium, ivy, acer and alpine strawberry leaves. Any interesting larger seeds I save, and I press and dry seedheads. A skeletonised leaf is a treasure and even small lacy fragments can be used. Autumn leaves can be most dramatic when displayed artistically on a collage and all sorts can be gathered and used. Interesting curved stems and tendrils will add grace to a collage and fine stalks can be used for baskets and posy stems. I always press lots of different herbs and almost always gather only the smallest sprays. Tiny sprigs of sage, mint, thyme, rue and rosemary are most appealing and I love blue borage flowers and greeny white Sweet Cicely umbels.

The various scented geranium leaves are elegantly shaped and retain their delicious perfume for a long time. Autumn-coloured ferns can colour most dramatically and they make lovely baskets. Grasses can look lovely when young and green or in their brown autumn colours.

I like to work with the miniscule pressed vegetables, and indeed slightly larger specimens too. Carrot thinnings are most appealing when pressed. Newly formed peas and beans, thinly sliced red cabbage, sliced okra, onions, baby sweetcorn, watercress sprigs, mustard and cress, alfalfa sprouts and slivers of globe artichoke are just a few of the vegetables worth experimenting with. Fruit, too, can be pressed. Sprays of alpine strawberries, slices of star fruit, halved and sliced tiny crab apples and slices of large strawberries will usually press well. Mosses and lichens are all useful, for their colours and textures are unique. If you live near the sea then the finer seaweeds can be gathered, washed and pressed. I use lots of berries which I lightly press or just dry. I always keep an eye open for interesting barks, particularly the paper-thin ones. Aromatic cloves, whole cardamom, star anise, allspice, peppercorns and pulses are all used on my collages.

There are lots of non-botanical ingredients that can adorn these small collages. When collecting seaweeds look for tiny shells and fragments of sea-glass. I have collected snippets of old decorative textiles for years and they yield beautiful old sequins, metallic threads and jet, glass and wooden beads. Old necklaces are strung with treasures and I love the tiny wooden beads of the 1920s and 30s that are often painted in dull metallic colours. It is now possible to buy narrow, pure silk ribbons and they tie into the softest bows for posies and bouquets, as do silk embroidery threads.

BACKGROUNDS

INTERESTING and imaginative backgrounds can transform the visual impact of any botanical arrangement. The backgrounds are just as important as the flowers, leaves, barks, seeds, mosses, lichens or even beads and shells that will be used to create the collage that will decorate a card. All the decorative and fine arts will fire one with inspiration, and the backgrounds and their textures and colours can become more intriguing than the actual subject matter of the work of art.

I have a large shallow florist's tray full of potential background bits and bobs. I dip into it randomly and find the most unexpected fragmentary strips of paper and card, ribbons, fabrics, threads, tubes of glitter and lustre powders, spray paints and a selection of watercolours.

All sorts of fabrics can be used and I love to experiment with striped ticking, scrim, linen, silks and satins or just any fabric that will create an interesting background and elevate a botanical arrangement from the mundane to the intriguing and artistic. All fabrics should be ironed on to self-adhesive fabric backing which will prevent them fraying when cut into shape.

Translucent watercolour washes on hand- or machine-made paper will add to the delicacy of posy and bouquet arrangements and give more importance to a single flower specimen. Thick matt watercolour backgrounds in both dull and brilliant colours can transform geometric rows of botanicals into fragments of an Indian textile or a scrap of Mexican folk embroidery; stylised arabesques of muted flowers and seedheads on a dark watercoloured background can be reminiscent of ecclesiastical brocade.

I am constantly discovering new ways to manipulate these paints and have recently been experimenting with 'antiquing' thick white paper. Simply immerse a large sheet of white paper in water until it is saturated (this usually takes about ten minutes). Remove the paper from the water and dab off any surplus water with a kitchen towel. The paper is then ready to be divided up into cards. It is best to divide the paper up into strips and divide the strips into card sizes – this facilitates the tearing process. Fold the paper gently along the measurement guidelines and carefully pull apart. This is quite easy when the paper is soft and wet, and the resulting edges have a most effective deckled edge to them. Whilst the cards are still damp, cover them with a diluted watercolour wash, paying particular attention to the torn edges of the paper where the wash should be well brushed in. Leave the cards for thirty seconds and then quickly rinse them under the cold tap. Most of the colour from the centre of the card will be washed away, leaving just a hint of colour around the edge of the card. Dry the cards flat. This antiqued paper creates an interesting background for all sorts of collages.

Fine tissue papers, gauzy Japanese papers and transparent Indian papers can all be covered with a diluted watercolour wash too. When they have dried, they can be torn into strips, rectangles and squares. The fineness of these coloured translucent papers has the quality of stained glass and all sorts of interesting effects can be created. Jagged-edged rectangles and squares can be ornamented with just one or two flowers, strips of a different length and colour can be joined to form coloured pennants and adorned haphazardly with flowers or neat rows of pressed vegetables, and even irregular scraps of discarded paper should be retrieved for they can become delicate landscapes for tiny flowers and seeds.

CARDS FOR
EVERY DAY

RANDOM FLOWER COLLAGES

Ingredients

Two folded blank cards 5¾ × 4¼in
(14.5 × 11cm) and 6¾ × 5in (17 × 12.5cm)

White card and watercolours

Black silk net

Spray glue and rubber-based glue

PRESSED BOTANICALS
BLUE CARD
Anemones, larkspur, lilac, grape hyacinth,
dicentra, pulmonaria, clematis, bluebell,
astilbe, borage, potentilla, hawthorn
berries, ribes, forget-me-not, columbine

RED CARD
Roses, clematis, maidenhair fern, potentilla,
bluebell, sterile blue hydrangea florets, astilbe,
crab apple blossom, akebia, grape hyacinth

O NE of the more unconventional ways in which I use pressed flowers are these 'random flower collages'. Once these collages are made they can be cut into squares, rectangles and strips and used in a variety of decorative ways. The background is important; in the past I have used skeletonised leaves but, exquisite as they are, they are not easy to come by, and I find pure silk net, dyed black or any dark colour, makes an excellent substitute. The cards are plain white machine-made paper.

RED CARD

1 Cut a 5¾ × 4in (13.5 × 10cm) rectangle from white card and colourwash it in scarlet.

2 Cover it lightly with spray glue and lay net over background, keeping the odd fold. Press onto background and trim excess away from edges.

3 Cut two long ¼in (5mm) wide strips of white card (at least 10in (26cm) in length). Colourwash one in scarlet and the other in royal blue.

4 On the background, arrange and glue botanicals, covering back of them with dots of glue ½in (1cm) apart. Group mixed blossoms fairly closely, leaving background exposed in patches.

5 Trim excess botanicals from edge of collage. Glue to front of smaller card, lining up left and lower edges of collage with left and lower edges of card.

6 Cut royal blue ¼in (5mm) strip to fit along top and right edges of collage. Cut scarlet strip to fit along top and right edges of blue strip.

BLUE CARD

1 On larger card draw a border of chevron stripes ½in (1.5cm) wide along top and right edges. Colourwash in sombre blue, mauve and pink.

2 Cut 6 × 4¼in (15 × 11cm) rectangle of white card and colourwash it royal blue. Attach net as in step 2 of red card.

3 Arrange a random collage of flowers on background as in step 4 of red card. Trim excess botanicals away from edges of collage and glue collage firmly in place on front of card.

❧ AUTUMN LEAVES ❧

Ingredients

Three folded blank cards 5½ × 3½in
(14 × 9cm)

❧

Yellow colourwashed, hand-torn
translucent paper 3 × 2½in (8 × 6cm)

❧

Green colourwashed, hand-torn translucent
paper 2½ × 2½in (6 × 6cm)

❧

Strips of colourwashed, hand-torn translucent
paper in yellow, orange and apricot
3 × ¼in (8 × 2cm)

❧

Autumn leaves

❧

Rubber-based glue

THESE autumn leaf cards rely on their backgrounds to give them a sense of style. Of course, the more one examines the leaves the more fascinating they become, but their impact alone is not strong enough to create a collage. However, when put against a background of delicately toning papers the leaves take on a new significance and their shape, colour and texture become visually more exciting. The diversity of leaf form is infinite, and searching amongst the dry autumn foliage can reveal the most unexpected treasures. In just a single foray you can collect enough leaves for a lifetime of card-making. However, part of the fun is to impose strict discriminatory rules when gathering and each leaf should be examined for a unique quality. But I still bring home far too many and the kitchen can become awash with leaves. I do, however, press them all and now have no need to gather

any more for years. I have used acer, *Rosa rugosa* and astilbe leaves here because I liked their colours and textures. The cards are simple cream hand-made paper.

ACER LEAF ON GREEN BACKGROUND CARD

1 Glue a handtorn green 2½ × 2½in (6 × 6cm) square of translucent paper to front of card, slightly above centre and position leaf on background.

2 Lift leaf and cover back with small dots of glue ½in (1cm) apart. Replace on background and press firmly into place.

ASTILBE LEAF ON STRIPED BACKGROUND

1 Glue in order from left to right one 3 × ¼in (8 × 2cm) strip of orange, two of yellow and one of apricot hand-torn paper to front of card, slightly above centre, as shown. Position leaf on background.

2 Lift leaf and cover back with small dots of glue ½in (1cm) apart. Replace on background and firmly press in place.

ACER AND ROSA RUGOSA LEAF CARD

1 Glue a hand-torn rectangle 3 × 2½in (8 × 6cm) of pale yellow paper and a hand-torn strip of darker yellow paper 3 × ¼in (8 × 2cm) on front of card, slightly above centre as shown. Position leaves on background.

2 Lift leaves and cover back with small dots glue ½in (1cm) apart. Replace on background and firmly press into place.

~ ORIENTAL CARDS ~

Ingredients

Three folded blank cards 4¼ × 3¾in
(11 × 9.5cm)
~

White card
~

Watercolour
~

Rubber-based glue
~

PRESSED BOTANICALS
GREEN CARD
Hydrangea paniculata
~

BLUE CARD
Fennel, fleabane
~

RED CARD
Spiraea

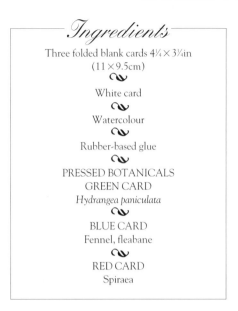

I FIND a lot of inspiration in the refined water-colours of Japan and China. My work usually displays a lot of detail and it is hard for me to leave any area unadorned, but my more recent interest in Oriental art has made me realise that the undecorated area on a collage can be as important as the decoration itself. Of course it has not been easy to come to terms with sparsely decorated collages, but they are growing on me and I am slowly finding more ways of adapting this elegant style to my own discipline. I have also found that these simple collages become even more Oriental in concept when divided into panels. Interestingly, nearly all my work can be cut into strips and re-assembled in whatever order, without detracting from its appeal in any way. The backgrounds used in these cards are colourwashed card that has been washed over for

a second time with diluted white watercolour. The effect that these backgrounds create is quite important and much of the collages' impact is lost without this diffused colour effect. The cards themselves are made from hand-made jute paper.

RED CARD

1 Cut out a rectangle of white card 3¼ × 3in (8 × 7.5cm). Colourwash in scarlet and allow to dry.

2 Colourwash in diluted white and partially rinse off under tap.

3 Arrange sprays of Spiraea across background as shown and glue in place.

4 Divide card into three equal sections longitu-dinally and mark with pencil lines. Cut along the pencil guidelines and glue the divided collage onto front of card, as shown.

BLUE CARD

Make as above card but use blue watercolour as the background and fleabane and fennel as botanicals.

GREEN CARD

Make as red card but use green watercolour as the background and *Hydrangea paniculata* as the botanical.

❦ FERN CARDS ❧

Ingredients

Three folded blank cards 5¼ × 3½in
(13.5 × 9cm)

❧

Selection of pressed ferns

❧

Rubber-based glue

❧

Fine draughtsman's pen

The Victorians were great fern collectors and had many varied decorative uses for them. Arrangements of pressed ferns adorned all sorts of household articles and I am particularly fascinated by their concept of decorating windows and glass doors with them. Although I have had an attempt at decorating a single pane of the kitchen window with ferns, it did not somehow look right, so perhaps I should remain with my pressed fern cards. The paper used for these cards is simple hand-made paper.

THE form and colour of pressed ferns are always beautiful, but it is better to gather and press only the smallest specimens as the larger leaves can be rather coarse. Newly emerging and unfurling fern fronds are particularly lovely with their elegant and unique shape. I prefer to arrange all my ferns together for I do not find that they are shown off to their best advantage in a mixed bouquet. Here in Cornwall the air is constantly moist and ferns proliferate in their thousands in our garden. Every few years I have a blitz on the terrace where the ferns seed in every available nook and cranny until there is no room for anything else. Up they all have to come, to be replanted in the less cultivated areas of the garden where they can run wild. I do have a wonderful selection from which to gather specimens in all their stages of development and wish that I had more use for them.

MIXED ARRANGEMENT OF FERNS

1 Arrange a small bouquet of mixed ferns on front of card.

2 Carefully lift ferns and cover back with small dots of glue ½in (1cm) apart. Replace and press firmly in position.

3 If desired, annotate card with fine draughtsman's pen.

MAIDENHAIR FERN CARD
Make as above card but use maidenhair fern.

BRACKEN AND MAIDENHAIR SPLEENWORT CARD
Make as for first card but use bracken and maidenhair spleenwort fern.

Ferns

P.B.
October '91

Ferns

P.B.
October '91

Ferns

Penny Black

❧ HERB CARDS ❧

Ingredients

Three folded blank cards: 6½ × 5¾in (16.5 × 14.5cm);
4¼ × 4in (11 × 10cm); 5 × 3½in (13 × 9cm)

❧

Colourwashed translucent paper 5¼ × 2in
(13.5 × 5cm)

❧

Pressed herbs

❧

Fine draughtsman's pen

❧

Rubber-based glue

I HAVE immense pleasure in growing the herbs that have played such an important role in the lives of our ancestors. Their visual appearance is of little importance, for it is their history that enchants me. I am fascinated by the vernacular names and love to use them whenever I can. Pressed herbs have a restrained elegance and I find their subdued colouring and delicate fragrance a delight to work with.

The three herb cards in this photograph are all quite different in style but the herbs themselves, no matter how they are displayed, will always retain their intrinsic aura of healing and alchemy. I like to have as many pressed herbs as possible and always ensure that I have pressed more small specimens than larger ones. Diminutive shoots, buds, sprigs, flowers, umbels, tendrils, seedheads and leaves are essential if one is to make delicate small collages.

The lavish fan-shaped display of mixed herbs has been arranged on textured oatmeal-coloured paper; the texture and ragged deckle-edge of the paper is in keeping with the natural feel of the herbs. I have used the same paper for the vertical herb arrangement. The creeping thyme card has a green colourwashed paper background which

is hand-torn, displayed on cream hand-made paper.

FAN-SHAPED HERB ARRANGEMENT

1 Assemble a large variety of pressed herbs. Build up herb collage gradually, arranging and gluing (small dots of glue ½in (1cm) apart on back of specimens) as the display develops.

2 Finish arrangement with central textured spike of herb flanked by two lateral sprigs of a prostrate herb.

VERTICAL HERB ARRANGEMENT

1 Assemble a large variety of pressed herbs. Arrange interesting specimens in a vertical design, leaving a central space for the annotation.

2 Lift botanicals and cover back with small dots glue ½in (1cm) apart. Replace botanicals on card and press firmly in place.

3 Using a fine draughtsman's pen, annotate herbs using either their Latin or vernacular names beneath the arrangement of herbs.

CREEPING THYME

1 Glue 5⅓ × 2in (13.5 × 5cm) hand-torn rectangle of green paper to front of horizontally folded card, positioning it slightly above centre.

2 Arrange sprigs of thyme, or any other prostrate herb, on background. Lift botanicals and cover back with small dots of glue ½in (1cm) apart. Replace and press firmly in place.

3 Using a draughtsman's pen annotate the herb beneath the lower edge of the coloured paper.

Mint, Lovage, Bistort,
Good-King Henry,
Royal Fern, Smallage,
Vervain, Thyme and Hops

Creeping Thyme (Thymus serpyllum)

BUTTERFLY AND MOTH CARDS

Ingredients

Folded blank cards: two 4½ × 3in (11.5 × 8cm)
and one 5 × 2½in (12.5 × 6.5cm)

White card and lustre powder

Sequins and black silk net

Rubber-based glue, PVA glue, spray glue

Fine stalks

Filaments of a peacock feather

PRESSED BOTANICALS
GREEN BUTTERFLY

Clematis viticella, Lobelia syphilitica, sterile
blue hydrangea florets, dock, angelica,
grape hyacinth

PURPLE BUTTERFLY

Potentilla, cyperus, *Buddleia globosa,* mimosa,
Lobelia syphilitica, elder flowers, rowan berries

MOTH

Gysophila, elder flowers, aster, rose,
callicarpa berries

W HO is not fascinated by the powdered lustre and exquisite patterning on the wings
of a butterfly, or the more refined markings on
the folded wings of a moth? I have wanted to
make stylised butterfly and moth collages for a
long time and these simple cards represent my
first attempt. Given time, I would like to do
some more as their form and ornament lend
themselves to glittering and jewel-like interpre-
tation. Sequins and beads could hob-nob with
textured flowers and berries on backgrounds of
lustre, glitter or even gold leaf. I have used rough
brown hand-made Indian paper for the cards.

GREEN BUTTERFLY CARD

1 Make a card template of butterfly 4in (10cm)
long and 1½in (3½cm) deep. Draw around template on white card and cut out shape.

2 Cover butterfly with a thin layer of PVA glue
and sprinkle on green lustre powder, tapping
gently to distribute powder evenly.

3 Arrange down centre of butterfly a column of
botanicals to form body and glue in place.
Arrange textured and flat botanicals in scant
decoration on outer wing edges. Glue in place.

4 Trim excess botanicals from edge of butterfly.
Glue onto front of horizontally folded card.

PURPLE BUTTERFLY CARD

Make as above using purple lustre powder.

GREEN MOTH CARD

1 Make a card template of a moth, 2½in (6cm)
long and 1½in (4cm) wide, as shown. On white
card draw around template and cut out shape.

2 Cover moth with a thin layer of PVA glue
and sprinkle on green lustre powder, tapping
gently to distribute powder. Lightly spray moth
with glue and press on net. Trim net from edges.

3 Using sharp scissors divide wings from back
to just below head. Arrange botanicals as shown
and glue in place. Glue sequins in place for eyes.

4 Trim away excess botanicals from edge of
moth. Glue moth in place on front of vertically
folded card. Glue two ¾in (2cm) lengths of peacock feather filaments for antennae.

Ingredients

Two folded blank cards 5½ × 3½in (14 × 9cm)
and 3 × 2½in (7.5 × 6cm)

White card

Lustre powder

Rubber-based glue and PVA glue

Pressed large round flowers (preferably
roses)

Pressed sprays

IF you are not used to manipulating flowers it can be quite difficult to create a well balanced flower arrangement. The flowers on these striking cards can be arranged to a pre-conceived plan and even if expertise is minimal, the resulting effect can appear professional. You are more limited as to the pressed flowers that lend themselves to a planned arrangement of this kind and I know of no other flower that would have the impact of the single dark red and pink roses. To make this arrangement more interesting it is important that the lower large blossom is only partially displayed, the remainder having been trimmed away level with the left-hand corner of the background. The two larger cards are hand-made cream paper and coarse hand-made jute paper. As none of the paper of the small card is visible I have used machine-made medium-weight paper.

MAKING BACKGROUNDS

1 Cut out three rectangles 3 × 2½in (7.5 × 6cm) from the white card and cover them with a thin layer of PVA glue.

2 Holding card level, sprinkle lustre powder on and tap gently to distribute powder. Tap background vertically to remove excess powder.

PINK LUSTRE CARD

1 Arrange roses in position on pink lustre background, ensuring pink rose is just tucked beneath red rose and the red rose extends over the bottom left-hand edge of the background.

2 Put medium dab of glue on centre back of each rose. Replace in position and press firmly in place.

3 When glue has dried, using sharp scissors trim off lower half of red rose level with background.

4 Where the roses do not overlap with each other, tuck behind the petals florets of pink statice on the back of which has been dabbed a couple of small dots of glue. Press florets in place.

5 Using an orange stick tipped with glue, apply two or three small spots of glue on the underside of the outer edges of each rose petal and press firmly in place. Using sharp scissors, trim statice level with edge of background.

6 Firmly glue decorated background in place on front of card slightly above centre.

GREEN LUSTRE CARD

Make as above card.

SMALL GOLD LUSTRE CARD

Make as other cards but glue decorated background firmly onto a small card the same size as background.

Penny Black

Penny Black

GILT BORDERED CARDS

Ingredients

Two folded blank cards 5¼ × 3¾in (13.5 × 9.5cm)

❧

Random flower collages (see p.20) measuring:
RED
Rectangle 2¼ × 4in (5.5 × 10cm)
BLUE
Rectangles 3 × 1¼in (8 × 3cm), 3 × ¾in (8 × 2cm),
1½ × 1¼in (4 × 3cm), 2½ × ¾in (6.5 × 2cm)

❧

White card

❧

Gold and silver leaf

❧

Writer's gold size

❧

Rubber-based glue

❧

Two 6½in (17cm) lengths narrow ribbon

WHEN making random flower collages it is best to decorate large pieces of card that can be cut up into various sized squares and rectangles. Here I have used strips of gold and silver leafed card to offset sections of random flower collage. The strips could have been covered with gold or silver paint, but occasionally I like to be extravagant and use the real thing. The paper is silky hand-made Indian paper.

RED AND GOLD CARD

1 Cut a long strip at least 12½in (32cm) in length of white card ½in (1cm) wide and colourwash it in strong brick red.

2 Paint a thin layer of writer's gold size over strip. Whilst the size is still tacky, but not dry (test every 15 minutes – usually takes 45 minutes) apply gold leaf by placing gold leaf tissue paper face down on tacky gold size. Fix gold leaf to sized card by rubbing tissue paper with a knife handle; this pressure will press the leaf onto the gold size where it will adhere. Remove tissue paper and if some gold still adheres to it, replace and rub again. It does not matter if the red shows as this adds to the 'antiqued' charm.

3 Glue random flower rectangle to front of card, slightly above centre. Surround the collage rectangle with strips of gold leaf, gluing in place.

SILVER AND BLUE CARD

1 Cut strip at least 16½in (42cm) in length of white card ½in (1cm) wide. Colourwash it in medium blue.

2 Paint a thin layer of writer's gold size over strip. Apply silver leaf to strip as for gold – see instructions for previous card.

3 Glue collage rectangles onto front of card ½in (1cm) apart, with wider rectangle on the left-hand side. Surround collage rectangles with strips of silver leaf, gluing firmly in place. Glue a strip of silver leaf between two rectangles.

GIFT TAGS

1 Cut two rectangles of white card, one 3 × 1¼in (7.5 × 3cm) and the other 2¼ × 1½in (5.5 × 4cm) and colourwash in medium blue.

2 Glue collage rectangles onto centre of colour-washed card. Using a thick needle, thread ribbon through centre of left-hand side of tags.

INDIAN TEXTILE CARDS

Ingredients

Three folded blank cards: two 5½ × 4in
(14 × 10cm) and one 6 × 3in (15.5 × 8cm)

White card

Watercolour

Rubber-based glue

PRESSED BOTANICALS
BROWN CARD
Lily of the valley, feverfew, fleabane, potentilla

MUSTARD CARD
Potentilla, separated ribes flowers,
hawthorn berries

ORANGE CARD
Fleabane, elderflowers, mimosa, potentilla,
separated ribes flowers

INDIAN textiles have played an important role in the development of my art. I have always liked the interesting and flamboyant colours of Indian embroideries and cloth and the repetitive and stylised floral designs that ornament these textiles. Watercolour backgrounds can create the colours of naturally dyed fabrics and botanicals can be arranged in the design of embroideries or native prints. These cards have been made from hand-made Indian paper and I love its curling deckle-edges; I never trim them for they are the signature of another ancient craft.

BROWN CARD

1 Cut rectangle of white card 3½ × 2½in (9 × 6.5cm) and colourwash in barely diluted brown.

2 Arrange columns of feverfew, lily of the valley and fleabane on background. Carefully lift botanicals and dab medium spot of glue on back. Replace on card and press firmly into place. Dot medium spot of glue on back of potentilla flowers and press on top of fleabane flowers.

3 Using sharp scissors, trim away excess botanicals from edge of background and glue background to card, slightly above centre.

MUSTARD CARD

1 Cut white card rectangle 3½ × 2½in (9 × 6.5cm) and colourwash it in sombre mustard.

2 Arrange columns of potentilla along both outer edges of background, flanked from within by separated ribes flowers. Lift botanicals and dab back with medium spot of glue. Replace and press in position. Cover back of hawthorn berry spray with small dots glue ½in (1cm) apart. Position in centre of background and press firmly.

3 Follow step 3 of brown card.

ORANGE CARD

1 Cut white card rectangle 4½ × 2in (11.5 × 5.5cm) and colourwash it in sombre orange.

2 On lower half of background arrange horizontal rows of elderflowers, potentilla and ribes flowers. Lift botanicals and dab back with medium spot of glue. Replace on background and press in position. Arrange fleabane and mimosa on top half of background. Lift botanicals and dab medium spot of glue on back. Replace and press in position.

3 Follow step 3 of brown card.

Penny Black

Penny Black

Penny Black

Greetings

COLOURWASHED
TISSUE PAPER CARDS

Ingredients

Five folded 'antiqued' cards 3½ × 2½in
(9 × 6.5cm) in dark pink, light pink,
mauve, green and orange

Colourwashed torn tissue paper rectangles
approximately 3 × 1½in (8 × 4cm) in dark pink,
light pink, mauve and two orange

Rubber-based glue

PRESSED BOTANICALS
DARK PINK CARD
Pink cow parsley, astilbe, clematis

LIGHT PINK CARD
Polygonum, rosebuds

MAUVE CARD
Polygonum, clematis

GREEN CARD
Clematis, fleabane, meadowsweet, potentilla

ORANGE CARD
Filipendula, potentilla

I HAVE had such fun making these cards. The design is new to me and I discovered it quite by chance. The artistry of these cards lies in the antiquing of the cards themselves, as described on p.16, and the use of colourwashed tissue paper. The pressed flowers would be of little visual importance without their stunning background. Using a small blank pale pink antiqued card and a scrap of pink tissue paper I arranged my pink polygonum and rosebud card in a matter of minutes. The others followed quickly and the only rule is that the base and left-hand side of the tissue paper should have a relatively straight edge. The other sides of the paper can then be as ragged as you wish – in fact this is part of their unusual charm.

MAUVE CARD

1 Glue a fragment of mauve colourwashed tissue paper more or less centrally on front of mauve antiqued card.

2 Arrange purple clematis and pink polygonum on background. Lift botanicals and cover back with small dots of glue ½in (1cm) apart. Replace botanicals and press firmly into position.

DARK PINK CARD
Make as above card using dark pink card and tissue paper, clematis, pink cow parsley and astilbe.

LIGHT PINK CARD
Make as first card using light pink card and tissue paper, pink polygonum and rosebuds.

GREEN CARD
Make as first card using green card, orange tissue, clematis, fleabane, meadowsweet and potentilla.

ORANGE CARD
Make as first card using orange antiqued card and tissue paper, pink meadowsweet and potentilla.

HIGHLY ORNAMENTAL CARDS

Ingredients

Three folded blank cards: two 5 × 3¾in
(13 × 9.5cm) and one 6¾ × 3⅓in (17.5 × 8.5cm)

White card and watercolour

Small beads and sequins in variety

Silver and pink lustre powder

Pink glitter and gold and silver spray paint

PVA glue and rubber-based glue

PRESSED BOTANICALS
PINK LATTICE CARD
Clematis, fleabane, rowan berries, rosebuds,
elderflowers, heather, polygonum, potentilla

PINK STAR CARD
Elderberries, fleabane, elderflowers, fuchsia,
polygonum, geranium, sterile blue
hydrangea florets, potentilla, deutzia

SILVER STAR CARD
Rosebuds, cow parsley, elderflowers,
Selinum tenufolium, clematis, polygonum,
green ivy berries, geranium

DEEP within my psyche there lurks a delight in all things theatrical. Occasionally I will participate in that compelling world. Out will come boxes of sequins and beads; flowers, berries and leaves will be gilded and silver-sprayed and ostentatious glitter will be liberally used. Only small botanicals can be used for the gold and silver effects must remain subtle. I have used creamy textured hand-made paper for the cards.

PINK LATTICE CARD

1 Colourwash rectangle of white card 6½ × 2in (16.5 × 5.5cm) black. Colourwash several strips of card ¼in (5mm) wide pink. Cover with rubber-based glue and sprinkle on glitter.

2 Cut the wide pink glitter strips in half lengthways to create two ⅛in (2.5mm) wide strips. Arrange thin strips in lattice design on black background as shown. Glue in position.

3 Spray some elderflowers in silver and some in gold. Lightly spray some elderberries, flowers and buds in gold. Edge lattice strips with beads, botanicals and berries, gluing as the design proceeds and using one small dot of glue on back of each. Leave lower half of background marginally incomplete.

4 Arrange botanicals in centre of lattices, leaving lower half incomplete. Lift botanicals and dab back with glue. Press into position.

5 Glue background to centre of card. Edge left and right side of background with a strip of glitter ¼in (5cm) in width and glue into position.

SILVER AND PINK STAR CARDS

1 Cut out a six-sided star approximately 4¾in (12cm) in depth and 3in (7.5cm) wide from white card. Cover in a thin layer of PVA glue and, holding horizontally, shake on silver lustre powder and tap gently to distribute powder. Hold vertically and tap to remove excess powder.

2 Lightly spray elderflowers, elderberries and other botanicals gold. Arrange botanicals on silver star, putting berries on last. Lift botanicals and dab with glue. Press in place.

3 Trim away excess botanicals from edge of star and glue star in place in centre of front of card.

STAINED GLASS WINDOWS

Ingredients

Three folded blank cards 7¼ × 2¾in
(18.5 × 7cm)

White card

Green, gold or silver lustre powder

PVA glue and rubber-based glue

PRESSED BOTANICALS
GREEN WINDOW CARD
Dock, bluebell, roses, potentilla, astrantia,
sterile blue hydrangea florets, pink yarrow

GOLD WINDOW CARD
Fleabane, geranium leaf, potentilla,
viburnum buds, feverfew, cotoneaster
berries, dock, clematis

SILVER WINDOW CARD
Potentilla, dock, cardamine, lilac, grape
hyacinth, roses, astrantia, sweet woodruff,
Cosmos atrosanguineus, spirea, clematis

Many of my collages, such as these window cards, are really like botanical embroideries. The paper is matt black watercolour paper.

GREEN WINDOW CARD

1 Cut an arched gothic window shape measuring 6¼ × 2¼in (16 × 5.5cm). Cover window with a thin layer of PVA glue. Holding window horizontally, sprinkle on green lustre powder and tap card to distribute powder. Hold card vertically and tap to remove excess powder.

2 Arrange on window, starting at the base, yarrow, astrantia, sterile hydrangea florets, potentilla and roses. Lift botanicals and dab on back one medium-sized spot of glue; on the hydrangea florets dab small spots of glue ½in (1cm) apart. Press in place.

3 Arrange vertical sprays of bluebell and dock on window. Carefully lift botanicals and cover back with small dots of glue ½in (1cm) apart. Replace botanicals and press into place. Trim away excess botanicals from edge of window.

4 On reverse side of window, pencil lines for panes of window, dividing it in half longitudinally and into three horizontally. Cut along pencil guidelines. Re-assemble, in correct order, on front of card and glue in place slightly apart.

GOLD WINDOW CARD

Make as above card using gold powder and different botanicals.

SILVER WINDOW CARD

1 Follow step 1 of green card, using silver powder.

2 Arrange on window, starting at base, roses, lilac, woodruff, cosmos, astrantia and grape hyacinth. Carefully lift botanicals and put one medium dab of glue on back. Press in position.

3 Arrange vertical sprays of dock, cardamine, spirea and clematis on window. Carefully lift botanicals and put small spots of glue ½in (1cm) apart on back. Replace botanicals and press firmly in position. Trim away any excess.

4 On reverse side of window, pencil lines for window panes, dividing it longitudinally into three. Cut along pencil guidelines. Re-assemble on front of card and glue in place slightly apart.

❧ LAVENDER AND ROSE CARDS ❧

Ingredients

Three folded blank cards – two 4 × 5¾in
(10 × 14.5cm) and one 4¼ × 5in (11 × 12.5cm)
❧

Two 7in (18cm) lengths of narrow ribbon
❧

Rubber-based glue
❧

Watercolour and fine draughtsman's pen
❧

PRESSED BOTANICALS
FOUR SQUARE ROSE CARD
Roses, rosebuds, rose leaves
❧

LAVENDER BOUQUET CARD
Sprigs of lavender, rosebuds
❧

LEAF, LAVENDER AND ROSES CARD
Roses, rosebuds, lavender spikes, double
chamomile, purple tellima leaf

A BOUQUET of roses and lavender is more tra-ditional than any other perfume. Since time immemorial the damask rose has scented our homes and ourselves and records of the use of lavender date back to the Greek and Roman cultures. My childhood memories are embalmed in the sweet scent of the roses that climbed over our cottage and the lavender that edged the path to the front door. I grow two small roses appro-priate for these cards – *Rosa multiflora* and the 'Threepenny-Bit' rose, *Rosa farreri persetosa*. I recommend growing the palest pink and white lavender as a bouquet of mixed lavenders looks most appealing. The cards are machine-made paper, cut with scissors.

FOUR SQUARE ROSE CARD
1 Using a draughtman's pen draw a double line border around the card ¼in (5mm) from outer edge. Divide the rectangle into four by drawing vertical and horizontal lines halfway inside line. Within the four rectangles, pencil another rect-angle just ¹⁄₁₂in (1mm) from border's edge.

2 Using a very diluted pink colourwash paint outside the double bordered frame to the edge of the card and within the four pencilled rectangles.

3 Decorate rectangles with roses, buds and leaves and glue in place. Annotate the roses.

LAVENDER BOUQUET CARD
1 Cut a ½in (1cm) strip off folded card from right-handed edge. Colourwash front of card in palest mauve and exposed edge in dark mauve.

2 Decorate edge with rosebuds and glue in place. Arrange sprigs of lavender and glue in place.

3 Tie two bows of ribbon and glue one on top of the other in the centre, where sprigs cross over. Lightly glue ends of bows in place. Write 'Lavender and Roses' on card.

LEAF, LAVENDER AND ROSES CARD
1 Draw a double line border around the card ¼in (5mm) in from outer edge. Using a pencil, draw a rectangle within the border just ¹⁄₁₂in (1mm) from the border's edge. Colourwash the rectangle in diluted blue.

2 Arrange the botanicals, cutting the leaf at the sides and lower edge as indicated. Glue in place. Write 'Lavender and Roses' beneath arrangement.

❧ GRASS CARDS ❧

Ingredients

Three folded blank cards 5½ × 3¾in (14 × 9.5cm)

❧

Pressed grasses

❧

Rubber-based glue

G RASSES can be gathered from almost any-where. Mid to late summer sees their flower and seedheads in infinite variety with cultivated and wild grasses in the garden; midsummer meadow grasses; hedgerows, verges and banks of grasses; shaded woodland grasses; cliffs of grasses and even exciting grasses that grow in the wet-lands. All the different species within the vast grass family produce quite individual flowers and seedheads and one could easily limit the orna-mentation of cards to include only members from this diverse group of plants. I have not pressed a great variety of grasses, but from the minimal selection that I do have, it was quite easy to make these different cards. I have used hand-torn and hand-made jute paper, the earthy colour of which blends beautifully with the brownish colourings of the grasses.

VERTICAL ARRANGEMENT OF GRASSES

1 Assemble grasses and, selecting those of a dif-ferent form, arrange a variety perpendicularly on the front of a card.

2 Lift up each specimen and cover back with small dots of glue, ½in (1cm) apart. Replace in position and press firmly in place.

FAN ARRANGEMENT OF GRASSES

Make as previous card, arranging grasses in a fan-shaped display.

CORNER DECORATED CARD

1 Assemble grasses and arrange textured florets of grass on all four corners of card.

2 Lift florets and cover back with small dots of glue, ½in (1cm) apart. Replace in position and press firmly in place.

3 Arrange small bouquet of similar grasses in centre of card. Lift each specimen and cover back with small dots of glue ½in (1cm) apart. Replace in position and press firmly in place.

Grasses

❧ FERN AND GRASS CARDS ❧

Ingredients

Two folded blank cards 5 × 3¾in (13 × 9.5cm)

❧

Tissue paper

❧

Writer's gold size

❧

Rubber-based glue and spray glue

❧

PRESSED BOTANICALS
GRASS CARD
Selection of grasses, skeletonised leaf

❧

FERN CARD
Selection of ferns

2 Cut a rectangle of tissue paper 4 × 3in (10 × 7.5cm) and paint it with gold size and allow to completely dry.

3 Spray back of skeletonised leaf with spray glue. Press firmly in place over rectangle of sized tissue paper and trim edges.

FROM early childhood I have been fascinated by detail. The finest stitchery captivates me, as does the anatomy of an insect or a posy of the most diminutive flowers. I find minute things have a unique appeal and I like to work with them. All my early pressed flower work used the smallest flowers, fronds, leaves and buds. I slowly progressed to larger things but given half the chance will return to my first love. These cards of the smallest grasses and ferns give me immense visual pleasure and although they are a fiddle to handle, even with forceps, I love to work with them. Grasses and ferns can be pulled apart into smaller sections and I like to arrange them in diminutive bouquets. I used transparent backgrounds of sized tissue paper and the cards should be propped where the light shines through the collage. The cards are simple hand-made paper and rough brown hand-made paper.

GRASS CARD

1 Cut a window 3 × 2in (8 × 5.5cm) in the front of the card.

4 On right side, using rubber-based glue, glue around edge of leaf-decorated tissue paper and place behind window on front of card and press firmly in place.

5 Arrange a small mixed bouquet of the smallest grass fronds on front of window and glue in place.

FERN CARD

1 Cut a window 3 × 2in (8 × 5.5cm) in front of card.

2 Cut a rectangle of tissue paper 4 × 3in (10 × 7.5cm) and paint it with gold size and allow to completely dry.

3 On right side (side that has been sized) glue around edge of tissue paper, place behind window on front of card and press firmly in place.

4 Arrange a small mixed bouquet of the smallest fern fronds on front of window and glue in place.

Penny Black

Penny Black

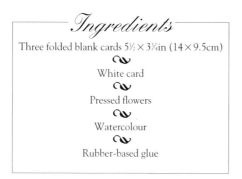

Ingredients

Three folded blank cards 5½ × 3¾in (14 × 9.5cm)
∾
White card
∾
Pressed flowers
∾
Watercolour
∾
Rubber-based glue

THESE simple flower cards are quite stark and rely entirely on a mixture of dark muted colours for their impact. The sombre water-coloured backgrounds are an interesting foil to the rather scant displays of botanicals, which are also quite muted in colour. Very few botanicals are needed for this type of card and the backgrounds in either monochrome or two-tone dingy colours are easy to prepare. The foxglove card was the first to be made. Due to their pouched flowers, foxgloves are difficult to press and I was particularly pleased with this specimen, where even some speckling on the pouches was visible. A section of any flowering stalk could have been used to make this card and of course the other two cards could have been

decorated with any available flowers and given different background colours. I have used simple cream hand-made paper.

FOXGLOVE CARD

1 Cut rectangle of white card 3½ × 2½in (9 × 6.5cm) and colourwash in barely diluted dark aubergine watercolour and allow to dry.

2 Cut 3½in (9cm) section from a foxglove spire. Cover back of specimen with small dots of glue ½in (1cm) apart and place specimen firmly in place on background.

3 Glue decorated background to front of card.

4 Draw ⅓in (8mm) wide border around deco-rated background and colourwash in sombre pale lilac.

BERGAMOT CARD

Make as above but colourwash background in uneven stripes as shown and use a single berg-amot flower as decoration.

FUCHSIA AND ASTILBE CARD

Make as above but use fuchsia and astilbe flowers.

Penny Black

Penny Black

Penny Black

MEXICAN-STYLE CARDS

Ingredients

Two folded blank cards – one 6 × 3½ in
(15.5 × 9cm) and one
3 ½ × 5¼in (9 × 13.5cm)

Strips of colourwashed tissue paper in
varying widths

Rubber-based glue

PRESSED BOTANICALS
HORIZONTAL CARD
Fleabane, pink-dyed statice, sterile blue
hydrangea florets, fuchsia, borage,
potentilla, pink larkspur

UPRIGHT CARD
Dandelion, buttercup, geum, forget-me-not,
rosebud, grape hyacinth

As with many of my collages, this style happened quite by chance. I believe the initial inspiration came from chalky bright pinks, turquoise, oranges and yellows found on Mexican ornamental crafts which I find so stimulating. I love mixing pinks and oranges, acrylic purples and blues and throw in a few fragments of glitter and lustre, and my idiosyncratic artistic satisfaction is gratified. I have days when I am compelled to work in these colours, and also when I have to wear them too!

I had at no time visualised these cards, but was just experimenting with strips of paper and brightly coloured and artificially dyed flowers, when suddenly they evolved. They appeal to me immensely and I shall experiment further, adding strips of glitter paper, some lustre powder and perhaps silver and gold gilt panels. I also have plans for larger collages and will no doubt have a field day with all my glittering and colourful ingredients. The cards are hand-made Indian jute paper.

HORIZONTAL CARD

1 Arrange strips of coloured torn tissue paper randomly, but keeping them vertical, and glue in place.

2 Arrange pressed flowers on tissue paper, as shown on card. Lift the flowers and cover the backs with small dots of glue ½in (1cm) apart. Replace the flowers on the card and press firmly in place.

UPRIGHT CARD

Arrange and make as previous card.

KLEE CARDS

Ingredients

Two folded blank cards – one 6¼ × 4¼in
(16 × 11cm) and one 5½ × 3¾in
(14 × 9.5cm)

❧

White card

❧

Gold paint

❧

Rubber-based glue

❧

PRESSED BOTANICALS
BOTH CARDS

*Vitis coignetiae, Vitis vinifera 'Purpurea',
parrotia, Acer pseudoplatanus 'Purpureum
Spaethii', Magnolia sargentiana*

THE geometry and colouring of much of Paul Klee's work has fascinated me for ages. His paintings reflect an imaginative law and order and his often sombre use of colour both soothes and intrigues my vision. The paintings fill me with ideas for collage work. Looking at the colourings of some of the autumn leaves this year I was reminded of Paul Klee's work. The leaves' leathery textures in shades of ochre, aubergine, russet, green-tinged-pink and plum were reminiscent of his painting *Choral and Landscape*. His painting and the autumn leaves filled me with ideas and I had to start work immediately on my version of a geometric collage, made entirely from strips, rectangles and squares of autumn bounty. I knew that the leaves would have to be reinforced in some way, and that to cut shapes of any size from them would entail only using the larger leaves. I glued them onto medium card so that there was no risk of them splitting or crumbling as I cut out my shapes. The paper of the cards is very rough hand-made jute.

STRIPED CARD

1 Using a pencil, draw on front of larger card a rectangle 3½ × 3in (9 × 7.5cm). Around the rectangle draw a border ⅛in (3mm) wide and paint it in gold.

2 Glue autumn leaves onto medium-weight card. Cut out five ½ × 3in (1 × 7.5cm) strips from leaves and one strip ¾ × 3in (2 × 7.5cm).

3 Glue the strips in place within the gold border, as shown on card, with the darkest strips at the top of the card, paling to the lightest strip at the bottom.

GEOMETRIC PATCHWORK CARD

1 Using a pencil, draw on front of card a rectangle 3 × 2½in (7.5 × 6cm) and a border ⅛in (3mm) wide around the rectangle. Paint border in gold.

2 Glue autumn leaves onto medium-weight card. Cut out ½in (1cm) wide strips from leaves.

3 Cut out a ½in (1cm) wide × 4in (10cm) long strip of medium-weight white paper and paint it in gold.

4 Using a Log Cabin patchwork design, as shown on card, arrange and cut strips of leaves and gold-painted paper and glue in place.

BOUQUETS ON CORRUGATED CARDBOARD

Ingredients

Two folded blank cards 4 × 6¼in
(10 × 17cm)

Corrugated cardboard

Rubber-based glue

8¼in (22cm) narrow cream ribbon

PRESSED BOTANICALS
BLUEBELL CARD
Bluebells, wild mignonette, whitebells,
white *Polygonum campanulatum*, *Clematis
recta*, grape hyacinth, dodecatheon, mitella

CLEMATIS CARD
Clematis viticella, lily-of-the-valley, dock

THE striped and rippled effect of corrugated cardboard can become an interesting background to a fragile nosegay of pressed flowers. The natural oatmeal colour and fabric of the paper blends perfectly with subdued botanicals, creating an air of refined simplicity. Pale whitebells and dodecatheon, creamy lily-of-the-valley, silky-tasselled *Clematis recta*, green wild mignonette, bluebells, grape hyacinths and the unusual black and grey pointed buds of *Clematis viticella* are all flowers with an unusual charm. When displayed against a quiet background, their elegant form and soft colouring are not overwhelmed. The bluebells will gradually lose their colour and fade to cream, as will the whitebells, but this does not matter for against their natural background they will still look pretty. In fact all the botanicals, with the exception of the grape hyacinths and *Clematis viticella*, will change colour, but I love the sepia hues that develop with age. Sometimes I like to work with only faded flowers, making collages reminiscent of the bleached dimities in old patchworks. The cards are finest cream hand-made paper.

BLUEBELL CARD
1 Cut out a rectangle of corrugated cardboard 2¾in × 5½in (7 × 14cm) and glue to front of card.

2 Arrange botanicals in a loose thin arrangement on corrugated background, ensuring that some extend beyond the edge either side and glue in place.

CLEMATIS CARD
1 Arrange a thin posy of flowers on cardboard background, crossing over stalks about 1¼in (3cm) up the stems and glue in place.

2 Tie a bow of cream ribbon and glue centre of bow in place where the stalks cross.

Penny Black

Penny Black

BASKET CARDS

┌─────────────────────────────┐
Ingredients

Two folded blank cards 4 × 5½in
(10.5 × 14cm)

❧

Corrugated brown paper

❧

White card

❧

Watercolour

❧

Rubber-based glue

❧

Agricultural peat pot, flattened

❧

PRESSED BOTANICALS
MIXED BASKET
Roses, rosebuds, white *Polygonum
campanulatum*, anaphalis, potentilla, dried
pink pepper berries, dried cotoneaster
berries, flower stalks, moss

❧

ANAPHALIS BASKET
Anaphalis flowers, flower stalks
└─────────────────────────────┘

SMALL wickerwork baskets were part of my childhood, when I filled them with freshly gathered mushrooms, blackberries, newly-laid brown eggs, marmalade sandwiches or flowery treasures from the woods. Tiny two-dimensional baskets make charming collages and can be made from moss, lichen, ferns, peat pots, over-lapping leaves, tiny bog myrtle cones, scented cloves or even an array of closely packed grass stalks. Massed blossoms of a similar variety can have almost more impact than a combination of different botanicals. I have put my basket on a background of corrugated paper which blends well with the brown hand-made paper of the cards, but almost any natural background would have been appropriate.

BASKET OF ANAPHALIS FLOWERS

1 Cut out background rectangle 4 × 3½in (10.5 × 8.5cm) of corrugated cardboard. Colour-wash with barely diluted dark blue watercolour and glue onto the front of a card.

2 Cut out peat pot basket 1½in (3.5cm) at base, 2½in (6cm) at top and 1½in (3.5cm) in depth.

3 Arrange on basket a latticed decoration of fine flower stalks, trimming them so that they do not project over edge of basket, and glue in place. Glue two thicker stalks horizontally above and below base and top of basket.

4 Glue basket onto background. Fill basket with anaphalis flowers, gluing as collage progresses, and working down from the top. Allow flowers to tumble over the top of the basket.

GREEN MOSS BASKET

1 Cut out rectangle 4 × 3½in (10.5 × 8.5cm) of corrugated card and glue to front of card.

2 Cut out basket from white card measuring 1½in (3.5cm) at base, 2½in (6cm) at top and 1½in (3.5cm) in depth. Glue moss to front of basket, entirely covering surface. Trim excess from edge of basket. Cover basket with lattice arrangement, as for previous card. Glue to background.

3 Gluing as the arrangement progresses, fill the basket from the top down, mixing buds, berries and flowers and allowing them to spill over the top.

ORNAMENTAL BORDER CARDS

Ingredients

Two folded blank cards 5 × 3½in
(12.5 × 9cm)

White card

Watercolour

Gold and silver paint

Rubber-based glue

Good selection of small pressed
botanicals such as:
Rosebuds, lavender, achillea, *Clematis
tangutica, Alchemilla mollis*, potentilla,
fleabane, feverfew, gypsophila, *Selinum
tenuifolium*, delphinium, geranium, elder
flowers, astilbe, polygonum, dock

M Y fascination with embroidery and needle-work manifests itself in all my botanical collages. For as long as I can remember I have collected fragments of embroidery and intricate sewing, snippets of ribbons, tapes and gimps and any old pieces of fabric or patchwork, regardless of condition, that reflect the dedication of a bygone era. These textiles are a constant source of inspiration and I apply their decorative charm to so much of my work. I gleaned the inspiration for these cards from a beautiful Log Cabin patch-work of Victorian embroidered ribbons. I colour-washed card strips of varying widths in all sorts of colours and then decorated them with botani-cals, ensuring that there was a repetitive theme to the design. I then arranged these pretty 'botanical ribbons' in a rather haphazard Log Cabin design, cutting them to the appropriate lengths. Each snippet of 'botanical ribbon' can be used and they mingle so delightfully regard-less of colour and design that it would be impos-sible not to make a success of these cards. Of course the borders themselves are quite painstaking to make, but once a good selection is to hand these most unusual collages can be assembled in just a few minutes. My cards reflect separate gold and silver themes, but they would have looked just as lovely mixing the metallic colours. These botanical patchworks have been glued onto the face of white machine-made paper cards.

GOLD AND RED CARD

1 Cut 6in (15cm) long strips of white card ¼in (5mm), ½in (1cm), ¾in (2cm) and 1¼in (3cm) in width.

2 Colourwash the strips in gold, silver, black, red, blue, green and purple or any selection of these colours. Put to one side one or two ¼in (5mm) and ½in (1cm) black strips which need not be decorated.

3 Decorate strips of colourwashed card with rows of pressed flowers and leaves, remembering to keep a repetitive theme.

4 Cut out rectangle of white card 3½ × 5in (9 × 12.5cm). On rectangle of card arrange dec-orated strips in a design similar to a Log Cabin patchwork, occasionally using undecorated black strips to highlight the design. Cut the strips to the appropriate length as the design progresses. Glue strips in place. Glue decorated Log Cabin rectangle to front of card.

SILVER AND BLUE CARD

Make as gold and red card.

COTTAGE GARDEN CARDS

Ingredients

Two folded blank cards – one 5¼ × 6¾in
(13.5 × 17cm) and one 4½ × 6in (11.5 × 15.5cm)

Brown paper and white card

Watercolour

Rubber-based glue

PRESSED BOTANICALS
WINDOW CARD
Moss, maidenhair fern, roses, astilbe, blue sterile
hydrangea florets, *Selinum tenuifolium*,
potentilla, double cardamine, grape hyacinth,
white *Polygonum campanulatum*, fuchsia

COTTAGE GARDEN CARD
Moss, lichen, potentilla, *Clematis tangutica*,
elder flowers, woodruff, anaphalis, pink
Polygonum campanulatum, feverfew, mitella,
maidenhair fern, astilbe, forget-me-not,
filipendula, geranium leaves, astrantia, fuchsia

I STARTED making these cottagey collages six years ago. They were my introduction into the world of decorative botany and for a period of time they were the only style that I could execute, having no desire to participate in the rather stylised pressed flower work that is fashionable. However, as my familiarity with pressed and dried flowers grew, so of course did my confidence, and I was able to experiment with other somewhat revolutionary ideas that were hatched as I worked away on my 'Cottage Garden' collages. My technique and style has changed a lot since those early days, but I retain a deep affection for this style. Almost all pressed flowers, buds and leaves can be used and small tufts of moss and lichen, if available, too. Although the impression may be of wild abandon, there is a positive structure and order to this style. Texture, colour, form, depth and height must be taken into account and it would be advisable to get a little practice before launching into these collages. My cottage garden card is really just three glimpses of my flower borders in high summer, crammed with both wild and cultivated flowers. The cottage window card carries through the same theme. The cottage garden card is made of fine beige hand-made paper and the window card is of white machine-made paper.

COTTAGE GARDEN CARD
1 Draw three horizontal pencil lines on front of card, 1½in (4cm) apart, from one side of card to the other.

2 Arrange a crowded display of botanicals along pencil guidelines, trimming their base so they lie level with guidelines. Glue in place.

COTTAGE WINDOW CARD
1 Cut out rectangle of white card 4 × 5¼in (10 × 13.5cm) and colourwash sky blue.

2 Arrange botanicals on blue background as shown on finished card and glue in place.

3 On back of collage pencil longitudinal and horizontal lines, halfway down and across card. Using sharp scissors cut along guidelines.

4 Cut background rectangle of brown paper 4¾ × 6¼in (12 × 16cm) and reassemble panes of window in centre of brown paper, leaving ¼in (5mm) gaps between panes. Glue in place.

5 Glue background to front of white card.

∾ BOTANICAL CARDS ∾

Ingredients

Three folded blank cards – 5 × 4in (13 × 10cm),
6 × 4in (15.5 × 10cm) and 2½ × 1¾in
(6 × 4.5cm)
∾
Brown paper strips 1½ × ½in (4 × 1cm)
∾
Fine draughtsman's pen
∾
Embroidery cotton
∾
Rubber-based glue
∾
Whole pressed plants
∾
Pressed flowers

As an amateur botanist I always like to examine every aspect of a plant's construction and growth. Flowers, buds, stalks, leaves and roots take on a new dimension when studied individually; one becomes more aware of the order of nature. Each component of a dissected flower is beautiful in itself and when displayed together they reinforce botanical knowledge. The inspiration for these botanical cards has been taken from the illustrations of early botanical books, where detailed and beautiful drawings illustrate the floral kingdom. The plants displayed on these cards are complete specimens, including their whiskery roots. On the cardamine card alongside the plant I have displayed a single flower, leaf and group of buds which add to the botanical interest of the card. The gift tag

was made in the design of a small card and I used flowering sprig of herbaceous geranium because I liked the purple flower and the interesting whiskers of the developing seed capsule. Any small plants are suitable for these cards. I have used simple cream hand-made paper.

CARDAMINE CARD

1 Arrange entire plant and separate flower, leaf and buds on card.

2 Lift botanicals and cover back with small dots of glue ½in (1cm) apart. Replace botanicals on card and press firmly in position.

3 Using a fine draughtsman's pen outline edge of 1in (4cm) long strip of hand-torn brown paper. Glue strip of paper alongside plant specimen and, using fine draughtsman's pen, annotate plant in Latin name.

VIOLET CARD
Same method as above.

GIFT TAG

1 Arrange flower on front of tag.

2 Lift botanical and cover back with small dots glue ½in (1cm) apart. Replace botanical and press firmly in place.

3 Thread a short length of cotton through top of tag.

Viola canina

Cardamine pratensis

SCENTED SPICE CARDS

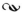

Ingredients

Two folded blank cards 5 × 4¼ in (13 × 11cm)
and 4¼ × 3½in (10.5 × 9cm)

❧

Unbleached hand-torn tissue paper
2½ × 2½ in (6.5 × 6.5cm) and 4 × 1½in
(10 × 4cm)

❧

3 in (8cm) narrow red silk ribbon

❧

Rubber-based glue

❧

Whole star anise, variety of spices, pressed
rosebuds, pressed scented geranium leaves

For a long time I have had an inclination to make large collages of interesting and varied spices. Not only would they smell delicious but the spices themselves would evoke the romantic flora of the Orient and New World. I have never succeeded with my large collages so I must content myself with decorating cards using the spices from my kitchen cupboard. It really does save a lot of time and trouble having the ingredients ready and waiting in the kitchen; no drying, gathering or pressing to be done, just the pleasure of arranging the little botanicals on a card. I feel that there is plenty of scope in this spicy field, but to date I have only had time to make a few cards. The spices used on these cards are cloves, cinnamon bark, star anise, anise seeds, allspice, coriander and lavender. I have included rosebuds and scented geranium leaves in my collages, but they could have been omitted. All these were the ingredients readily available to me, but other spices could have been used. The card paper is quite primitive and its surface and deckle-edges are littered with tousled fibres; I love it and find it borders my tiny spice collages most appealingly.

LARGE SPICE CARD

1 Glue hand-torn 4 × 1½in (10 × 4cm) tissue paper rectangle to front of horizontally folded card.

2 Arrange spices on background and position scented geranium leaf and rosebuds.

3 Lift botanicals and cover back of spices and rosebuds with medium dab of glue and other botanicals with several small dots of glue ½ in (1cm) apart. Replace botanicals on background and press firmly into place.

SMALL SPICE CARD

Make as above to step 3. Tie narrow red silk ribbon around the star anise and attach to the top of the card.

TICKING CARDS

Ingredients

Two folded blank red cards 6 × 3¾in
(15 × 9.5cm)

Interfaced ticking 3½ × 2½in (9 × 6.5cm)

Black watercolour

Rubber-based glue

Small flowers, buds, berries

M Y inspiration for these cards comes from the ticking work embroidery of the eighteenth century, with the black stripes of the ticking making an ideal background for floral embellishment. The flowers, buds, berries and leaves that I have have used adorn the ticking in the style of the rich Middle Eastern embroideries of the past, creating interesting mosaics of colour. The more diverse the collection of small jewel-coloured botanicals, the more freedom there is to create flamboyant and rich designs. I never work to any pre-conceived plan or design, but just let my instincts guide me and the most unlikely designs and colour combinations evolve. On these cards large and small rosebuds, potentilla, feverfew, polygonum, astrantia petals, mimosa, clematis buds and elderberries decorate the ticking but the selection is endless. The paper I have used is light-weight red card, cut with scissors.

1 Assemble a variety of small jewel-coloured botanicals.

2 Glue ticking background to front of card slightly above centre.

3 Arrange botanicals and glue in place a row at a time, using a medium dab of glue to fix them to the ticking. Press firmly in place.

4 Around the decorated ticking background rule a pencil border ⅛in (3mm) wide. Colour-wash it with barely diluted black watercolour.

STILL LIFE CARDS

Ingredients

Two folded blank cards – 4½ × 6¾in
(11.5 × 17cm) and 5 × 6¾in (13 × 17cm)

~

White card

~

Watercolours

~

Gold leaf and gold spray

~

Rubber-based glue

~

PRESSED BOTANICALS
BLACK JUG CARD
Alchemilla mollis, lilac 'Sensation', sterile blue
hydrangea florets, roses, potentilla, pink
Polygonum campanulatum, gold laced primroses,
fennel, elder flowers, dried cotoneaster berries

~

TURQUOISE JUG CARD
Pink gypsophila, roses, potentilla, sea
carrot, sterile blue hydrangea florets, elder
flowers, *Clematis tangutica*, woodruff, fennel
leaves, maidenhair fern, pink cowparsley,
bougainvillea, woody nightshade

I HAVE been interested in the fine arts for a long time and love to browse through my many books on the artists I most admire. Many ideas for my work have blossomed from the seeds sown within my subconscious by the inspired work of others and the natural landscape. When I made these still life cards, with their unusual decorative backgrounds of strident colours, I was following my own inclination. However, I was recently looking at some paintings and collages by Matisse, whose colours, subject matter and techniques have always fascinated me, and was suddenly aware that my inspiration really came from his work. The cards are white machine-made paper.

BLACK JUG CARD

1 On front of larger card pencil guidelines for separate sections of background and colourwash.

2 On white card draw handled jug 3½in (9cm) high and cut out. Colourwash matt black. On white card cut out small pot 2in (5cm) high and cover with gold leaf, as per instructions on p. 34.

3 Arrange botanicals on different background sections, as shown, and glue in place, leaving background bare where the jug and pot will be. Position jug and pot and glue in place. Decorate jug with elderflowers and glue in place.

4 Arrange the flowers and berries in the jug, as shown, and glue in position as the collage progresses, starting at the top and working down so the botanicals spill over the lip of the jug.

5 Fill gold pot with potentillas in same manner, and glue in place. Trim away any overhanging botanicals from the edge of the card.

TURQUOISE JUG CARD

1 On smaller card pencil rough guidelines for separate sections of background and colourwash. On white card draw and cut out jug as previous card and colourwash turquoise.

2 Arrange botanicals on different background sections, as shown, and glue in place, leaving the background bare where the jug will be.

3 Position jug on background and glue in place. Decorate jug with gilded elder flowers and other botanicals. Fill jug with botanicals and glue in place as for black jug.

VEGETABLE AND FRUIT CARDS

Ingredients

Three folded blank folded cards 5½ × 3¾in
(14 × 9.5cm)

Colourwashed translucent paper, hand-torn
into strips

Fine draughtsman's pen

Rubber-based glue

PRESSED VEGETABLES
Carrots, okra, beans, green tomato, baby
sweetcorn

PRESSED FRUIT
Crab apple

ALL the pressed vegetable and fruit cards have a unique fascination. No one seems to associate fruit and vegetables with pressed botanicals but many of them press extremely well and, what is more, when cut into longitudinal and cross sections, they become an academic study in botanical structure. You do not necessarily need a garden or the countryside from which to gather these ingredients – a visit to the local supermarket will offer a cornucopia of ideas. Pressing fruit and vegetables is a matter of trial, error and expertise. Not everything will be a success but all failures will add something to the storecupboard of experience. The smallest fruits and vegetables press into the most appealing botanicals – a newly formed French bean or seedling carrot has infinitely more refinement than its mature counterpart, so always try to acquire the smallest specimens unless the fruits and vegetables are to be sliced into sections.

SEEDLING CARROT CARD

1 Carefully glue two hand-torn strips of orange paper on the front of the card, as shown.

2 Arrange a selection of miniscule carrots on and between the paper strips. Lift the carrots and cover their backs with small dots of glue ½in (1cm) apart. Replace in position and press firmly in place.

3 Using a draughtsman's pen, annotate the card.

VEGETABLES ON A COBWEB BACKGROUND CARD

1 Carefully glue a square of hand-torn, green translucent paper on the front of the card.

2 Arrange a longitudinal section of okra, two tiny carrots, newly formed beans, a cross section of a small green tomato and a section of baby sweetcorn. Lift the vegetables and cover their backs with small dots of glue ½in (1cm) apart. Replace in position and press firmly in place.

3 Using a draughtsman's pen, annotate the card.

CRAB APPLE CARD

1 Carefully glue a small rectangle of hand-torn, green colourwashed paper to the front of the card, as shown.

2 Arrange a thin section of pressed crab apple in the centre. Lift the apple and cover its back with small dots of glue ½in (1cm) apart. Replace in position and press firmly in place.

3 Using a fine draughtsman's pen, annotate the card, as shown.

Crab Apple   Jenny Black

French Beans, Tomato,
Sweet Corn, Carrots,
Peas and Okra.   Jenny Black

Carrots   Jenny Black

FLOWER POT CARDS

Ingredients

Two folded blank cards 5½ × 3¾in
(14 × 9.5cm) and 4½ × 4in (11.5 × 10cm)

❧

Peat pot

❧

Rubber-based glue

❧

Watercolour paint

❧

Fine draughtsman's pen

❧

BROWN CARD

Potentillas, lilac, geraniums, *Polygonum campanulatum*, rosebuds, grape hyacinths

❧

TURQUOISE CARD

Blackberries, pink pepper berries, callicarpa berries, sterile hydrangea florets, rosebuds, pink-dyed gypsophila, maidenhair fern

I HAVE always loved growing my flowers in pots. Crammed with herbs and geraniums, they filled the window ledges and porches of the country cottages of my childhood. Flower pot cards have this same rustic appeal, and can be filled with any flowers, seeds, berries, spices, pulses, mosses or lichens available. They are quick and easy to make and their endearing quality always arouses admiration.

BROWN POT CARD

1 To make the brown pot, carefully flatten a horticultural peat pot and cut out of it a small pot approximately 1½in (3½cm) in height and ¾in (2cm) wide at the base. Using the roughest side of the pot as the right side, very lightly glue it in place about one third of the way up the blank folded card.

2 The pot can now be filled with flowers and buds. Starting at the top of the arrangement and applying one or two small blobs of glue to the back of the botanicals, arrange the flowers and buds in place. Tuck some blossoms slightly behind others and spill the arrangement over the top of the pot. Press lightly in place.

3 Using a fine draughtsman's pen, annotate the botanicals used, keeping the writing around the base of the pot.

TURQUOISE POT CARD

1 To make the turquoise pot, cut out a small peat pot measuring approximately 1in (2½cm) in height and ⅔in (1½cm) wide at the base. Colourwash the pot using barely diluted cobalt green paint. When it has dried, lightly stick it halfway up the blank card.

2 Beginning at the top and using very little glue, gradually build up a textured arrangement of berries, flowers and buds. The arrangement should cover the top of the pot.

3 Finally, to balance the collage, arrange a rosebud and a sprig of sterile hydrangea blossom either side of the pot.

Penny Black

Potentillas
Lilac
Geraniums

Polygonum
Roses
Grape Hyacinth

Penny Black

August 1991

'OLD HERBAL' CARDS

Ingredients

Two folded blank cards 5 × 4in
(13 × 10.5cm)

Rubber-based glue

Brown paper

Fine draughtsman's pen

PRESSED BOTANICALS
Blue columbine, mousetail plant

O F all the cards in this book, the botanical ones are the easiest to make. Even the most humble weed becomes fascinating when isolated from its environment and displayed on a card of hand-made and hand-torn paper. Artistic arrangement is unnecessary as all one needs to see is a precisely arranged botanical specimen which has been clearly annotated with its Latin name. The charm of these cards is in their simplicity, reminiscent of a page from an old herbal. I generally like to use common or garden weeds for this type of card, but occasionally I will be tempted by a rarer plant that has a unique form, or perhaps an old-fashioned flower that has a particular association for me.

If you wish to evoke a feeling of the past with these cards, it is essential that the paper resembles the hand-torn paper of the early herbals. Hand-made paper is an obvious choice, but machine-made paper can look old and full of character when the edges have been torn rather than cut. The cards in this photograph have been made with textured hand-made paper.

COLUMBINE CARD

1 To make the small card, cover the back of the flowers, buds and stalk of a pressed blue columbine with smallest dots of glue and position them carefully on the card.

2 Using a draughtsman's pen, write the plant's Latin name on a strip of hand-torn brown paper. Edge the label with fine black lines and glue alongside the flowers.

3 Finally, draw a fine black line at the top and bottom of the card just above and below the torn edges of the paper.

MOUSETAIL CARD

The mousetail card is made in a similar manner, using a larger piece of card and omitting the fine black rules.

Arisarum proboscideum

Aquilegia Alpina

BINDWEED WRITING PAPER
AND CORRESPONDENCE CARDS

Ingredients

Blank torn-edged writing paper 9 × 6in
(23 × 15.5cm)

Torn-edged correspondence cards 4 × 5in
(10 × 13cm)

Rubber-based glue

PRESSED BOTANICALS
Lesser bindweed

SHOULD the day ever come when I have time on my hands, then I will certainly make and decorate my own writing paper and correspondence cards. Large sheets of hand-made paper are quite widely available these days and they are not expensive, particularly those imported from the Third World. A sheet measuring 20 × 33in (50 × 85cm) will make approximately nine sheets of writing paper and quite a few assorted sized correspondence cards. These cards and sheets of writing paper can be hand-torn to size and decorated with the most humble wayside weeds. In fact one could easily make this botani-cal stationery without even being the possessor of a garden.

I am fascinated by the organic lines of the lesser bindweed and, when pressed, it becomes a delicate art nouveau decoration. The intertwining stems and sagittate leaves have been of inspiration to the artist for centuries and, when using the actual pressed plant, it resembles a fine watercolour. If I was not constantly tempted by the heterogeneous plant world I could do no better than to decorate all my stationery with the common or garden lesser bindweed. The paper is creamy textured, hand-made and Indian.

WRITING PAPER

1 Arrange tendrils of lesser bindweed in top left hand corner.

2 Carefully lift the botanicals and cover the backs with small dots of glue ½in (1cm) apart. Replace and press firmly in position.

CORRESPONDENCE CARDS

Follow the writing paper instructions, but use a smaller bindweed specimen.

LARKSPUR WRITING PAPER AND ROSY LETTER CARD

Ingredients

Hand-torn sheets of writing paper 6¼ × 9in
(16 × 23cm)

Hand-torn correspondence cards 3¾ × 5in
(9.5 × 13cm)

Hand-torn letter card 8 × 10in (20 × 25cm)

White card and double-sided adhesive tape

Rubber-based glue and PVA glue

PRESSED BOTANICALS
WRITING PAPER AND CARDS
Pink larkspur, goatsbeard

LETTER CARD
Rosebuds, rose leaves

A LL stationery is quick and easy to make and very few pressed flowers are needed. However, some artistry is required for the decorations must appear to be at ease with their background. I always press goatsbeard before it is fully out while the fronds are still apple green. Their colour blends beautifully with pastel-shaded flowers and they can often replace leaves. The letter card is an unusual way of folding paper and it requires no envelope to be sent through the post. I have painted these botanicals with a diluted solution of PVA glue and this will ensure they remain intact when handled. All the papers used are cream and hand-made.

WRITING PAPER

1 Arrange botanicals on paper and glue in place.

2 Dilute ½ teaspoon PVA glue with 1 teaspoon water and, using a fine brush, paint over botanicals.

CORRESPONDENCE CARDS

1 Arrange botanicals on cards, and glue in place.

2 Paint botanicals with diluted PVA glue.

LETTER CARD

1 Cut out card template 7 × 3¼in (17.5 × 8.5cm) and place on sheet of writing paper as shown.

2 Fold paper around template in order of 1, 2, 3, 4 and then turn paper over and turn over small flap 5 over top face of letter card.

3 Decorate small flap with botanicals and glue in place. Paint over botanicals with diluted PVA glue.

4 Cut ¾in (2cm) strip of double-sided tape, remove one layer of covering and fasten on inside of flap 5. This will keep letter closed in the post.

Happy Birthday

Greetings

Greetings